Little Books of Leadership

Also in the series:
Resilience
Crisis Leadership by Margaret Benefiel

COMMUNICATION

COMMUNICATION

A little
book of
leadership

CHURCH
PUBLISHING
INCORPORATED

This book compiles text from the following sources:

Church Wellness: A Best Practices Guide to Nurturing Healthy Congregations by Tom Ehrich

Re-membering God: Human Hope and Divine Desire by Tobias Stanislas Haller, BSG

God with Skin On: Finding God's Love in Human Relationships by Anne Robertson

Leaders Who Last: Sustaining Yourself and Your Ministry by Margaret J. Marcuson

Tweet If You Heart Jesus: Practicing Church in the Digital Reformation by Elizabeth Drescher

Community Rules: An Episcopal Manual by Ian S. Markham and Kathryn Glover

Unabashedly Episcopalian: Proclaiming the Good News of the Episcopal Church by Andrew Doyle

Church Publishing
19 East 34th Street
New York, NY 10016
www.churchpublishing.org

Cover design by Jennifer Kopec, 2Pug Design
Typeset by Progressive Publishing Services

A record of this book is available from the Library of Congress.

ISBN-13: 978-1-64065-407-5 (pbk.)
ISBN-13: 978-1-64065-408-2 (eBook)

Contents

A Word about the
Little Books of Leadership

The deepest roots of the word *lead* mean "to travel." Other meanings of the word have to do with guiding, showing the way, and conducting, all of which carry a sense of movement: we are on our way to somewhere or something.

In the church setting, that sense of movement lives in creative tension with the institution and the pull of self-preservation. We are people with a deep history and a compelling present tense; we are also a people with a complicated past and an uncertain future. We are always looking for a leader—someone who helps us navigate the journey.

The models of leadership in our present society are myriad. The ones that get the most attention have too often been those that are more directive than collaborative, more authoritarian than inclusive. If we listen closely, we can hear what the apostle Paul called "a gong or a clanging symbol." Leadership that is not based in love rings hollow.

The Little Books of Leadership are an ongoing series designed to offer points of contact and conversation to congregations as they live out the daily journey of what it means to be God's beloved community. To say there is no one-size-fits-all approach is to state the obvious, yet we can learn from one another's stories of what has been done and left undone. We can listen for new rhythms of the Spirit and change how we conduct ourselves in our life together.

Jesus said those who wished to lead had to learn how to serve if they were going to be effective, which is to say, we are called to attend to one another and respond accordingly. To lead in such a fashion is, to borrow a favorite Episcopal phrase, to travel the Way of Love.

Come, let us travel together.

Introduction

It is difficult to understate the importance of communications.

Our faith is grounded in "Word"—the desire of God to communicate with humanity—and the ministry of Jesus was an exercise in communications. From beginning to end, he taught, healed, served, died, and rose again in ways that brought people closer to him and to God, that enabled them to see beyond the immediate, and that were intended to form community.

As our world has grown more complex and noisier, the task of communications has become more critical. We require information in order to live effectively. We must learn to process information in order to make wise decisions. We must learn to discern and to assess information in order to maintain our freedom and integrity.

The tools of communications have grown more sophisticated, interesting, and powerful, but so has competition among users of those tools, including those who use effective communications to intimidate, to prey, and to lead us astray.

The healthy church will accept the critical importance of communications, adopt the best possible strategies and technologies for communicating effectively, and stop wasting resources on communications that don't work. We must care as much about what we say and how we say it as Jesus did.

The communications environment has changed dramatically over the past fifty years, leaving many churches stuck with costly and ineffective communications tools. The environment continues to change as new technologies emerge and people's lives change. The most significant change, of course, is the emergence of the internet as a primary tool for communications. That tool, in turn, changes daily.

The current internet-centered communications environment is a "level playing field," meaning that any organization can set up an effective website at a reasonable cost and use e-mail and messaging. Moving away from ineffective tools such as print-on-paper newsletters can save a substantial amount of money. The bad news is that a level playing field rewards only those who play effectively. The stakes are high. A congregation that refuses to embrace new technologies will find itself invisible.

Communications, in other words, epitomizes the critical nature of "best practices." But alongside the technology and tools, communication is fundamentally about relationships: community, conflict, competition, cooperation, consensus. We have to be aware of both intent and impact as we try to live out what it means to be the body of Christ in today's world. What follows in these pages are different aspects of communications from theology to practice, from general to specific. The more we understand one another, the more we are able to share the love of Christ.

1 ▪ Communication Starts with Community

The first sign of the Spirit's presence with us is *community,* for the Spirit *calls* and *summons* us, drawing us together, or rather *back* together, re-membering us as members of the church so that we can re-member God together. The Pentecost narrative does not end with the apostles going out to the four corners of the earth with their newfound language skills. Rather, it ends with them gathered in an even tighter and yet growing community, one that holds all things in common and, most importantly for my theme, a community that worships together in the temple and gathers in fellowship for the breaking of bread and prayers.

Community, then, is one of the great markers of the Holy Spirit's presence: for a gathered group of many to be in and of one spirit. There have always been great souls who have gone it alone, great saints whose solitary encounter with God is the stuff of legend and sacred history. The saints of yore number among them the spiritual athletes who encountered God flying solo, out in the wilderness, like Moses and Elijah, or the Egyptian Desert Fathers and Mothers, some of them going so far as to live solitary lives in caves or on the tops of pillars, as far away from human society as they could get. We cannot neglect mention of the great anchored solitaries of the Middle Ages, especially Julian of Norwich, who chose a path not entirely cut off from human society, but one that maintained a clear though porous separation from "the world" and the worldly. There is a difference between solitude and isolation: Donne reminds us that no one is ever entirely *isolated*, that is, no one is "an island"—however separate those in solitude may appear to be, they are promontories of the main body, not cut off from it.

However, unlike such rare souls as Moses and Elijah or the Desert Fathers and Mothers or the solitary anchorites, most of us will not find God in solitude, but in *community*. God does indeed appear to isolated spiritual athletes like Moses or Elijah in a burning bush or a still, small voice. But if *we* are spiritual athletes, it is much more likely to be as players on a team.

Moreover, the Holy Spirit appears to favor the public assembly over the private audience. The disciples were in the same place *together* when the Spirit came upon them, and the Spirit, far from driving them apart, bound them even more closely together by the end of the account. The Spirit came upon the apostles not in the midst of them pursuing their own individual holiness, but while they were praying together, for and with each other. It was at that moment the Spirit blew through the windows and set their souls on fire. And in that moment they became, in one way, what they *were* and what they *were meant to be*. A single atom of carbon cannot fulfill its purpose alone, though it has certain characteristics that allow it to fulfill those purposes when joined with other carbon atoms in the form of graphite, coal, or diamond, or with other elements as part of a living thing. So it is that community is the engine that realizes identity, that makes of us what we are and are meant for. And it is in community—from the most intimate community of a loving couple, to the humble gathering of two or three in Jesus's name, to the wide community of the church—that the Spirit comes to us, revealing Christ in our midst, and revealing us, re-membered, as his body.

When Christ is revealed among us, he shows himself foremost as one who *serves*, who before his death washes the feet of his friends and afterward responds to their betrayal and lack of belief with words of peace, who offers them forgiveness so that they might be able to forgive in turn. This service and forgiveness find their natural home in community. For just as it takes two to tango, it takes two to serve, two to forgive. Service and forgiveness flow *from* community as naturally as dance flows from music, when you simply have to move your feet to the persuasive beat.

The ministry of hospitality, which combines service and mercy and grows from community, is the second sign and verification of true communal spirit, the second sign of the Spirit's presence: "see how they love one another" is Christ's identity badge for the church, both for those within and for those outside. We will know each other by our love, and others, seeing that love, will know the presence of the Holy Spirit among us.

We see the emergence of this in the passage from Acts, as the concern for the welfare of the group leads to communal sharing of goods, the gracious and fluid distribution of abundance in the direction of need, as natural as waters flowing downstream to be joined in the great sea.

Hospitality, that flow of grace to need, takes many forms: in a parish coffee hour or visit to a shut-in; in a welcome assist with an unfamiliar hymnal; in the round of prayer the convent offers, in which the visiting guest is gently folded in as neatly as a prayer card in a breviary; in an act as simple as an outstretched hand to help someone on the steps to the altar or as formal as the baptismal rite itself with its welcome into the household of God. Our Acts account ends with the growing household of the church, and we continue to offer a hospitable greeting to each newly baptized person, welcoming them into a dwelling for the Spirit whose building stones are the church's members.

Do you remember the children's game "Here is the church, here is the steeple, open the doors, and see all the people"? The outside of a church looks like a building, but when the doors are opened, the living, human construction is revealed—as a community. So hospitality is both the *beginning* and the *fulfillment* of the community we call the church. It is the first thing that the church is *for*. The disciples were gathered when the Spirit came, and the Spirit knit them closer together, adding to their number day by day as they worshiped, prayed, and served.

But let's back up a bit. There is something else to note in our account, and this is the part that, because it *does* get read each year, suffers from familiarity. The first response the apostles made to the Spirit's arrival was to proclaim the story of salvation to each other in many languages, so that those outside the house were attracted by the sound and were astonished to recognize their mother tongues, the languages of their first birth. That recognition would lead some three thousand of them to the second birth of baptism, incorporation into the body of Christ. Thus the Holy Spirit of God sets Babel on its head. Those who in ancient days *didn't* want to be scattered, who made their own city's survival the be-all and end-all of their efforts, who assaulted heaven with a proud tower so that they might *make a name* for themselves, were given the curse of tongues to *divide* them. But on Pentecost, the gift of tongues serves to do exactly the opposite. It undoes the fragmentation of Babel and calls people back together from the four corners of the earth. The Spirit graciously runs the film backward so that all who once were scattered are now called back together through this same multiplicity of language, not to make a name for themselves, but to give honor, praise, and glory to the one Name under heaven and upon the earth by which we are saved and to take on that Name in baptism: not to build a tower as an anchor for self-generated human unity, but to find salvation in the strong tower of Jesus Christ, lifted high to draw the whole world to himself.

On that day of Pentecost, the Holy Spirit gave the gift of language to the gathered apostles. And of course, what they said is as important as the languages in which they said it—the medium was not the sole message, though it served to catch the ears of the visiting multitudes. But it was the *proclamation* of God's saving deeds that ratified the Spirit's presence, a powerful sign of God being with those who spoke. The children of Israel knew this well, that the *proclamation* of the saving story is a constituent part *of* the saving story, and they were always telling that story to each other. Even in captivity, even when they complained they couldn't possibly sing a song of Zion as their captors demanded, their very confession of incapacity to sing became itself a song (Psalm 137), a chorus of memory to fallen Jerusalem, a making-present of Zion even by the waters of Babylon, a warning to their captors of coming judgment, and a recollection and new chapter in their story. And their story sustained them through that exile and captivity in Babylon, that antitype of fabled Babel, and it supported them and held them together through and beyond the destruction of the Second Temple, and even up to this day, through and beyond the most terrible and single-minded effort to exterminate them since they were formed by God as a people.

The proclamation of the story of salvation, what we might call the Haggadah of Israel, has been the spiritual life stream that has preserved this people. The Christian church's story is added to theirs, a supplement and not a replacement, and each of us has a story too, like footnotes and annotations expanding the history of salvation, so that the whole world could not contain the books that might be written.

However, "the world" that confronts us today is a world where community is shattered, dismembered, unremembered: a world that doesn't know how to serve, a world that has forgotten its own story. The world will not stop talking long enough to hear the gracious possibility offered to it. Well, the world needs a wake-up call. And the responsibility to give that call falls on us, the members of the church, the body of Christ: to re-member, to welcome, and to tell the story of salvation to the world.

Every Christian community—every parish, every religious order, every prayer fellowship, every outreach group—can be an icon of community, hospitable service, and proclamation. By faithfully gathering as the fellowship of the apostles gathered, by faithfully praying as the apostles prayed, by faithfully continuing to break the bread of life day by day and week by week, by opening their doors in hospitality so that starved souls can flee the plenty of the world for a time and feed on that seemingly sparse but truly abundant bread of life, by sharing the goods of the world for the good of the world, especially with those who have less, by telling the story faithfully to each other and to all who have ears to hear: by doing these things, the parishes and communities and groups can be focal points for the Spirit's action, tinder for the sparks to light, ground for the Spirit to shake and rock the world to its foundations and recall worldly humanity to its true identity.

If all who are pledged to do so faithfully continue to proclaim that story, the world might stop its chatter for a moment and overhear: that's how it worked on Pentecost, and it can work again. People who have forgotten that they are God's children, in the midst of the bustle of great and terrible cities, in the sometimes desperate and lonely quiet of the countryside, in the coldly subdivided patchworks and culs-de-sac of the suburbs—people hungry for God's word might suddenly hear a voice speaking a language they haven't heard for a long, long time, but that they recognize at once: a language from home, reminding them who, and *whose*, they are.

We who are pledged to welcome the stranger as we welcome Christ can open our doors and our hearts and welcome them in, and in so doing we will be magnified. Together we will offer glory to God such as has never rung from the corners of the world where God has been pleased to plant us.

If we who are pledged to the common life in Christ can truly live into the spirit of community that finds its home in the very heart of the Triune God, we will by the Spirit of God send forth from our communities such ripples of grace as will echo through the dismal alleys of the cities and over the rolling hills of the countryside and sweep aside the neatly subdivided principalities of the suburbs.

The Spirit reveals Christ's presence in the gathering of the community, in the service and hospitality that they share, and in the telling of the greatest story ever told. But the Spirit also reveals Jesus to us through a fourth sign unlike any other: in broken bread and a cup of wine. I will reflect on this wonderful gift at greater length in a later chapter, but I would not be true to my text if I omitted at least a passing reference to it here and now. It is in the breaking of the bread, in the fourth sign of the Spirit's presence, in the eucharistic feast, that the servant reveals himself to be the bridegroom, the guest reveals himself to be the host, the stranger met wandering alone on the open road is shown to be the heart and soul of all community and fellowship. And the story takes a classic and surprising turn: like Richard the Lionheart casting off his pilgrim's cloak to reveal the king's bright red cross on his chest to an astonished Robin Hood and his band, who drop to their knees. The king has returned!

Suddenly, though the doors be locked, we realize who has been standing among us all this time, and we can hear his breathing. Suddenly the Holy Spirit descends upon us and upon these gifts, and we remember and are re-membered into the body of Christ, and in this act re-member God. Once one special Pentecost, the Spirit gathered the apostles together like a harvest of grain once scattered on a hillside. And gathered together they served and proclaimed and feasted. The many were one in fellowship, in the breaking of the bread, and in prayer and service. We, their successors, can do no less, especially given our baptismal commitment to this precious ministry. This is, after all, our *liturgy*, our *work for and as the people of God*. This is what worship is for; this is *who* worship is for. We have been called together and consecrated for a purpose: Christ our Passover is sacrificed for us, and the Holy Ghost our Pentecost has come to us. So come, let us welcome; come, let us proclaim; and come, let us celebrate the feast.

2 ▪ Staring Down the Competition

Competition is everywhere in the Bible. Right out of the gate we have the snake pitting God against Adam and Eve in the quest for knowledge. "Eat this fruit and put yourself on a level playing field with God," he says in effect. "Even the odds. God is just trying to quash competition by forbidding you to eat." Of course, we know how that turned out. The first siblings competed in their offerings to God and it resulted in the first murder.

We've already seen in detail the competitive rivalry between Jacob and Esau and saw how God turned competition on its head by throwing the wrestling match by the Jabbok River. There's the smack down between Moses and Pharaoh, Elijah and the prophets of Baal, Israel and its neighbors, kings and those who would supplant them. Things are no better as we turn to the New Testament. The disciples argue among themselves about who is the greatest, and the earliest Christian communities were developing a competitive my-founder-is-better-than-your-founder spirit, forcing Paul to respond, "What then is Apollos? What is Paul? Servants through whom you came to believe, as the Lord assigned to each" (1 Corinthians 3:5).

Paul certainly spends a lot of ink trying to get those first churches to realize that they were not separate entities in competition with each other but rather "we, who are many, are one body

11

in Christ, and individually we are members of one another" (Romans 12:5). Perhaps recognizing our competitive nature, Paul tries to steer it in another direction a few verses later saying, "outdo one another in showing honor." It is interesting that back in studies of competition between friends, the category of competition that has the least detrimental effect on the friendship for both men and women is altruism—when friends tried to outdo one another in doing good for others.

Certainly, Paul uses competitive metaphors in his letters saying, "Do you not know that in a race the runners all compete, but only one receives the prize? Run in such a way that you may win it" (1 Corinthians 9:24). Overall, however, it seems that Paul would at least like to redirect our competitive spirit to things that serve the Kingdom. He collects money for the poor in Jerusalem and praises the relative giving of other churches to get people to give generously. He trumpets his own righteousness compared to others but then follows his boast with, "Yet whatever gains I had, these I have come to regard as loss because of Christ. More than that, I regard everything as loss because of the surpassing value of knowing Christ Jesus my Lord" (Philippians 3:7–8a).

The clearest examples, however, come from the Gospels. Very early on a rivalry begins to stir in the hearts of the disciples of John the Baptist. John has been the big game in town, with crowds flocking to him to be baptized in the Jordan. But Jesus sets up shop downstream, and John's disciples come to him saying, "Rabbi, the one who was with you across the Jordan, to whom you testified, here he is baptizing, and all are going to him."

John responds with incredible grace. "The friend of the bridegroom, who stands and hears him, rejoices greatly at the bridegroom's voice. For this reason my joy has been fulfilled. He must increase, but I must decrease" (John 3:29–30). John the Baptist is the one sent to prepare the way for Jesus. Many might point to his calls for repentance and baptism as the way in which he did that. He prepared the way for Jesus by showing that, in the kingdom of God, the rules are different. In the Kingdom, you win by losing, thus destroying the spirit of competition. Think about it. Competition can't exist if nobody is trying to win and if nobody wants to be seen as better than somebody else. But does the Bible support the desire for win-win? That's not what John the Baptist is saying. "He must increase, but I must decrease" is not win-win. John is saying that he will lose willingly and then be truly happy in the win of another. It's not about everybody winning. It's about robbing the word "win" of any meaning by being eager to lose.

That also seems to be the approach of Jesus. When the disciples argue about which of them is the greatest, Jesus presents a child and says, "for the least among all of you is the greatest" (Luke 9:48), or as the version in Mark 9:35 has it, "Whoever wants to be first must be last of all and servant of all." That's not exactly the competitive spirit.

Lest the point be lost, when Jesus gathers with his disciples in his final days, he gets up from dinner, ties a towel around his waist, and washes the feet of his disciples as a servant would do. That of course upsets the apple cart, especially with Peter, who is still very certain that important people should have privileges that others do not. Jesus explains by emphasizing both his prominence and his servanthood: "You call me teacher and Lord—and you are right, for that is what I am. So if I, your Lord and teacher, have washed your feet, you also ought to wash one another's feet. For I have set you an example, that you also should do as I have done to you" (John 13:13–15). Jesus was not caught up in a need to win.

Just a quick word search shows that the word "win" appears in the Gospels only once. It is in Matthew 23:15 where Jesus is blasting the Pharisees for traveling far and wide to win converts and then perverting the message. By contrast, Jesus uses the word "lose" thirteen times. Paul, on the other hand, uses "win" ten times and "lose" only twice. It's not a scientific study, but perhaps that's why so many churches like to stick with Paul and approach the words of Jesus only with reverent caution. We do not like to lose. We would much rather "fight the good fight" (1 Timothy 1:18) and "finish my course" (Acts 20:24) than to take seriously "If any want to become my followers, let them deny themselves and take up their cross and follow me. For those who want to save their life will lose it, and those who lose their life for my sake will find it" (Matthew 16:24–25).

It appears that Jesus does not promote competition or model it as a way of life. Since we believe that Jesus is the revelation of God—meaning that we can understand the nature of God by observing Jesus's life—the absence of competition in the life of Jesus tells us that it is also absent in God. We do not have to compete for God's affection. God does not prefer winners and condemn losers. The picture Jesus gives us of God's MO is that our salvation is a cooperative effort. God ties a towel around his waist and serves human beings, encouraging us to do that for each other. Instead of racing each other to the finish line, we link arms and move in fits and starts toward the goal, stopping every time someone falls behind to help them back on the road. And when all of us come upon a chasm that not even the most agile of us can jump, God lies down across the breach so that we can move on. Love is not about who wins.

When we live our lives competitively, it is easy to carry that worldview across to our faith. If salvation is a competition, some must win and others must lose. If God loves the winners, then we must hide our sins deep rather than bring them to the surface in repentance. If God is competitive, then it is right to pray that we win the war or even the football game. If God loves the winners and condemns the losers, then so must we. But if God keeps messing up competition by throwing the game—becoming a servant even though he could be a king, dying on a cross instead of conquering Rome, saying that the wealthy ones are those who give everything away—then our worldview looks a bit different. What if Kingdom life is about cooperation rather than competition?

If that's the case, God is not smiling when we push out our chest and run through that finish line ribbon. God might just wipe the grin off our faces, turn us around, and send us back six miles to help the one with a pulled hamstring. God might not be pleased that we never missed a Sunday in church if we used our weekly attendance to smugly put down those who only came on Christmas and Easter. We might get to the pearly gates far ahead of the pack, only to find that no one is allowed in alone.

Being God with skin on for our peers means putting aside our competitive instincts to be sure that everyone succeeds. Keeping the proprietary information will enhance us personally, but in the Kingdom, those who are first get sent to the back of the line. If you're smarter than your classmates, help them study for the tough exam. If you can see a solution to your competitor's problem, offer it. The Formula 1 racing study shows that while your own company may not be as far out in front, the larger business community will thrive. And isn't it better for all of us if there are many companies adding jobs and contributing to the GDP?

As Christians, our lives are supposed to be a witness to God's nature. In professing that Jesus is our "Lord," we are saying that our actions reflect his rule and his preferences for how life should be lived. Jesus makes it quite plain that being his disciple means living very differently from the world. In this case, it means giving up on entering the "rat race," the competition with others for life's toys and resources. There is no drive to keep up with the Joneses in Kingdom life. Like Paul in Philippians 4:12, we learn to be content with what we have. We don't seek to be proven better than others in competition. We take whatever gifts we have been given, tie them around our waists, and use them to serve others.

In our churches, it means that we are not in competition with the church down the street or with the other service in our own church on Sunday morning. When they grow, we rejoice because more people are finding their way to faith. We support their ham and bean supper, even if they never cross the threshold of our church fair. In our own congregations it means recognizing that even though you've been given the baritone solo in the Christmas Cantata every year for fifteen years, the new guy with the amazing voice really does deserve to have it. "He must increase, I must decrease," must become something we are capable of saying in recognition of the gifts of others.

In doing so, however, we can't let ourselves fall back into thinking that we have "lost" and are therefore less in God's eyes. God is incapable of seeing either a winner or loser. As Paul says in Galatians, "We are all one in Christ Jesus." In Paul's metaphor we are one body with many members. It's not about whether the right eye is better than the left leg. It's about whether they are each healthy and doing what they are gifted to do. A church can do several things to decrease a spirit of competition more than by engaging everyone in discovering their own spiritual gifts and then working to deploy them in ministry. To be God with skin on for our peers means helping them to see themselves as God sees them. They are not losers. They are not winners. God is not interested in where they stand relative to anybody else. God merely wants them to wake up to their role in the body and fulfill that function to the best of their ability.

The studies show that if we take even seemingly innocent competition out of our relationships, we will have a healthier response to conflicts. We won't get as much personal recognition as we might otherwise receive, but industry-wide, the human industry will thrive. By elevating the concept of losing, Jesus threw the game. He refused to compete and, in doing so, saved us. "For I have set you an example," Jesus said after washing their feet, "that you also should do as I have done to you."

3 ▪ Building Relationships

Leadership never happens in a vacuum but rather among specific individuals in a particular context, which means we need to relate to them. Building these relationships is like building capital we can draw on when we want to challenge people to move forward in some new ways. If we do not take the time to make these connections, any changes we institute will be short-lived and will certainly not last beyond our tenure. The force for human togetherness is a powerful one, and leaders ignore it at their peril. In any church, large or small, we must be well-connected to key players and find ways to communicate with everyone. Preachers, of course, have the pulpit, but it takes more than preaching to forge a solid connection with a congregation.

At the same time, leaders are not just one of the gang, and they have to be prepared to step apart from the group. Leaders have to be able to deal with the loneliness that ensues; we all want to be accepted, and it is hard to move apart. Find the balance between connecting with people and stepping ahead of them to lead is the ongoing dance of community life. The content of our ideas and the course we chart are critically important, but we need to pay attention to our relationships. They determine the outcome of our leadership endeavors as much as our direction. The best leaders balance individuality and togetherness, moving ahead while fostering close ties with their followers. This is called "differentiated leadership," and at its most basic, it involves maintaining ourselves and staying in relationship with those around us.

Leaders need to find the right balance between closeness and distance. You cannot minister or lead in isolation. Still, solitude is necessary: you do need the time alone to think and pray. Yet, then you need to come back into the fray, to connect with all the people: the ones you love as well as the ones who drive you up a wall. It is not easy to find this balance in relationship. We have all known leaders who were too close to their followers. The need to be liked drives many of their decisions, or they are simply unaware of the need for boundaries. They lose perspective on their position. Ultimately, they become ineffective because they are unable to take a stand. Clergy sexual misconduct may be the most extreme example of getting too close in congregational life. But a pastoral leader who simply avoids conflict by never taking a stand may also be too close. And a priest whose entire social life revolves around the congregation may have trouble finding enough distance to lead. We have also known leaders who were too distant. A rector under stress may spend more and more time in the office, doing administrative work and preparing sermons. They attend meetings but leave as soon as they are done. They avoid those who are critical, even as anxiety increases, but by doing so jeopardize their ministry. Another priest may use denominational involvement as a way to distance from a parish the priest feels unsuited for. Or a minister distracted by family worries may not have the energy to connect appropriately. In all these cases, being too distant from the parish makes leadership difficult because the substantive relationships to support it are not there.

Finding the balance between too close and not close enough takes energy and attention and creates two related challenges: first, to lead without taking on the anxiety of others. This does not mean we never listen to the worries of our people. It does mean we work to be clear on which worries belong to us and which do not. Others will be glad to hand us their anxiety, which can keep us from responding thoughtfully. For example, if a parishioner is upset about a change in worship, he or she may want us to do something immediately. But if the change is part of a long-term strategy, worked on with the vestry, the leader's task simply may be to keep talking with that member, to keep the relationship going while we continue to move forward with the strategy.

Second, we need to lead without trying to will people to be different. This does not mean we do not have opinions or a point of view on the direction the congregation should move. But it does mean we acknowledge and respect differing points of view, giving people room to have their own opinion. Even when we must make a decision from the top, those decisions will work out better when we put in the time on relationship building and when we do not willfully try to convince them of our perspective.

Integrity in leadership means not simply doing the right thing, but more fundamentally having boundaries: knowing where we end and other people begin. As we work on our relationships, we relate to others with respect and expect the same respect in return.

Developing relationships in congregational life means we see this connection as part of our job. We intentionally devote time to it and think strategically about how to make connections happen. There are as many ways to do it as there are leaders, but all leaders must do it.

All leaders need to find their own way of connecting. This is not simply a management or leadership technique. The best leaders find out how to relate to others in a way that fits them and in a way that fits their context. A church setting calls for a different kind of connection than does a business. For a pastor who loves it, pastoral visitation can be a wonderful way to connect, even in today's fast-paced world. For another leader, a regular routine of phone calls to the vestry to check in at least monthly might serve the same purpose.

We can try out different ways to connect, but if we try to use techniques, people sense phoniness and resent it. We may strategize for ways to develop relationships, but, finally, we have to be as fully present as we can with the people we lead. We have to show up, breathe, look them in the eye, and say what we really believe. Leadership is about *how* we say it, as well as *what* we say. When we are truly present with people, they know it. When we are on autopilot, they know it. Over time a dynamic relationship develops, and trust increases. We learn their cues, and they learn ours. As a leader, we are part of an ensemble cast, and the give and take contributes to the whole. They cannot do it without us, and we cannot do it without them.

The presence of leadership is such that it makes itself known. A leader does not need to make a personal connection with every individual in order to be engaged with everyone. In larger organizations this is impossible. But the leader's presence still matters, no matter how large the system. In a large church, the senior leader has to think constantly about how he or she is maintaining a presence with the entire congregation. This is equally true of a bishop or executive in a denomination. Maintaining a presence is far more than a communication strategy: it is a way of thinking about the nature of leadership that can affect everything a leader does. We must think through how we are maintaining our connection with those with whom we may not have a one-to-one relationship. Consider where we need to show up in person, by e-mail, or by phone in order to make this happen.

When leaders are thinking about relationships, they will act in different ways and make different decisions. For example, a rector could decide to attend the choir Christmas party even though it makes December even busier. Another pastor might prioritize phone messages and e-mail, not according to the content of the message or the emotional tone, but based on the way the pastor wants to connect with the congregation. The pastor would take time to think before responding automatically to anxious messages.

Staying connected to others in a mature way means being ourselves in relationship to them. We work to do this without being pulled into a comfortable harmony where we all have to agree. When we have to agree, there is not much opportunity for progress. This is a temptation for church leaders because often we were socialized to be nice. A lack of conflict is viewed as a good thing by both clergy and congregations. But it can get in the way of growth.

To pull apart from the crowd and take a clear stand can mean that we upset people, but when we put in the time building relationships, it is easier to move through these difficult times. Leadership in a congregation takes time; building these relationships takes years. The first thing is not vision, but relationships. The challenge over time is to take a stand and watch the reactivity heat up, manage yourself, and tend the relationships.

We need to distinguish between relationship process and short-term problems in the relationship: the reaction to Sunday's sermon, the budget shortfall, the disorganized youth director. Such problems demand our attention and often we do need to respond quickly to the anxious e-mail regarding last week's sermon, to the budget problem, or the matter of staff incompetence. But looking only at the content of the problem is not enough.

Paying attention to process means we are watching the overall pattern of relationships in the congregation, including our part in the pattern. We notice what happens when we or other leaders take a clear stand, no matter what the issue: who jumps on board immediately, who can be counted on to automatically disagree. We learn enough about the history of the congregation to assess how the relationship patterns in the present reflect the past. Perhaps people in this parish have always been critical of the rector's preaching. Maybe the person holding the job of youth director never does very well, no matter who it is, and perhaps we have contributed to this. It can be a challenge to manage ourselves and relate to others when anxiety is high. When people are angry, fearful, or critical, we may be inclined to withdraw, to hide, or to go on vacation. But when we can stay in touch, the potential for a good outcome increases. More than any specific events, the leaders' response to those events helps determine outcomes. Leaders who keep their heads and do not panic can often keep small conflicts from spiraling into big ones.

Relationships get tested in every aspect of congregational life: worship, music, youth program, staff dynamics, letting staff go, denominational conflict, cutting the budget, or increasing the budget. We can easily get focused on the content of any of these issues and seek to argue rationally with people until they agree with our position. Or we can avoid conflict as much as possible and hide our own views. Neither of these approaches will be productive.

Instead, the tasks are these: first, put all our energy into clarifying and articulating what we ourselves think on the one hand (without trying to convert anyone to our point of view), and second, keep building relationships. This is the path of self-differentiated leadership. When we follow this path, people will intuitively know we are respecting them, and they will be better able to hear what we are saying.

And while the leader needs to stay on track with their goals, adjusting direction in response to feedback is also essential. Staying on course doesn't mean we can't adjust the course in response to those with whom we are making the journey. Congregations made up of mature people can weather the inevitable ups and downs rather than splitting apart or dwindling away. Instead, people are committed to their own growth, to each other, and to the health of the congregation and its work.

We need to know how to manage the balance between closeness and distance from others. We all grow up in families that to some degree do not know how to do this right. In our family we learn about relationships and develop our instinctive responses to others. Some families are very good at closeness but do not know how to be separate. Some families are very good at distance but do not know how to be close. Understanding our own process and what it is we do in relationships will help us relate to others.

There is real potential for pain in relationships in congregational life. We actually have to increase our tolerance for our own pain in order to grow. We need to tolerate people being angry or disapproving of us and to deal with our discomfort at relating to them. Working on relationships is as much about us as it is about the other people. We play a part in all our difficult relationships. We want to blame the other, but it always takes two for there to be a problem, and we need to be honest enough to look at how we play our part.

Time to reflect is essential, along with some outside help to discern our own patterns of behavior. When we become anxious, do we withdraw or become more aggressive? Do we go numb? Do we shut down or start talking too much? The more we observe what we do, the better we can relate to people in congregational life, both those we find easy to relate to and those who seem more difficult. We cannot make a different choice if we do not know what you do. Whatever our leadership position, knowing and managing ourselves will benefit us more than anything else we do.

The same principles apply to all levels of leadership. If we are leading a ministry area, we must work on developing key relationships with others in that area. If we have a boss, we must work on that relationship as diligently as we can.

We can also work on some clarity about our own bottom line—what we will and will not put up with. For those in the middle, this is particularly important if the top leader either wants peace at any price or is a hostile force. The conflict-avoidant leader may be just as dangerous as the unpredictable and autocratic one. Having a bottom line, clear boundaries, and multiple options is critical. Thinking through options and having an exit strategy—whether we use it or not—can be useful for any leader and can free us up for more creative thinking about the challenges at hand. If we feel like we have to stay, we will feel stuck and find it harder to be flexible and imaginative. If we see options, we will feel freer and be better able to contribute to our own area of ministry and to the whole life of the parish.

We are also in relationship with those leaders who have gone before and those who will come after us. The author of the letter to the Hebrews refers to the great "cloud of witnesses" that surrounds us as we "run with perseverance the race that is set before us" (12:1). Keeping that fact in mind can help us maintain perspective on the progress we have made. If we feel we are lagging behind, perhaps it is because we are facing challenges bequeathed to us by our predecessors. If we feel we are doing well, it is in part due to the strengths of those who went before. If we are starting something entirely new, we can remember our hopes for those who come after and start thinking about the future and planning for succession.

As in a relay race, the leadership handoff is important. Transitions from one leader to another are key times for any institution. When we are leaving, we can be aware of our own vulnerability to loss and transition—wanting to hang on too long, or wanting to get out as quickly as possible, or wanting to make our mark as soon as possible.

Entering a new system requires the same rigorous attention.

We make more progress when we focus on our own functioning, without blaming others who have gone before us or feeling like we must measure up to a glorious past. Our task is to pay attention to our own part in the story right now. We should not get distracted from the steps we need to take today. This does not mean we ignore those who have gone before. We can look for times to invite living predecessors back to connect the institution with the ongoing race. We ask about stories that need to be told, to give ourselves and others energy to keep persevering. Obstacles overcome in the past may inspire us in the present. The story does not end with us. Occasionally reminding ourselves and everyone else that our tenure is not forever can help those we lead to dream big about the future and to become less dependent on our leadership. And it can help us keep perspective on the place of our own leadership in the whole story of the congregation's ministry.

4 ▪ Practical Considerations

We Are All Family . . .Some of Us Are Friends

We don't choose family. Family is a given. Through Christ's death and resurrection to new life, God has made us all brothers and sisters in Christ, which means there is a kinship, an obligation to honor and be there for each other. But like all large families, we are closer to some siblings or relatives than we are to others, perhaps because of shared interests or a shared stage of life. This is not surprising, and it is okay. We honor the entire community of the church and aspire to recognize the kinship we have in Christ, while we are also allowed to enjoy spending time with particular people.

Everyone Has a Part to Play in the Body of Christ

Paul, writing to the church in Corinth, offers an inspired image of the church: it is the "body of Christ" (1 Corinthians 12:12–27). Every part of the body is needed. The foot is as much a part of the body as the hand; and the eye cannot say to the hand that the hand is not needed. Paul's powerful image captures Christian community: everyone is indispensable and valued. Everyone has a ministry by virtue of our baptism. All roles are important, especially those that are less visible. We are all called by God to find our role and to play that role.

Never Be Afraid to Apologize

We all make mistakes—sometimes by design, sometimes inadvertently. Admitting our mistakes through an apology is an acknowledgment of our own humanity and fallibility. It invites others to see and know us more fully and invites them to be more fully themselves. Being reconciled to each other is a Christian obligation. Jesus says, "So when you are offering your gift at the altar, if you remember that your brother or sister has something against you, leave your gift there before the altar and go; first be reconciled to your brother or sister, and then come and offer your gift" (Matthew 5:23–24). It is never too late to apologize. Sometimes waiting gives the other person time to be readier to hear and accept the apology. Be sincere, straightforward, and clear about the reason for the apology.

Learn to Forgive

Just as we are called to apologize to others for our words and actions, we are also called to forgive those who apologize to us. We honor ourselves and the other when we forgive. Both the apology and the act of forgiveness are ways of dealing with the past: they are ways to make sure that true community can be restored. The wrong has been acknowledged, and the wrong has been forgiven. The author of Ephesians explains that we forgive each other because God forgives us in Christ: "Be kind to one another, tenderhearted, forgiving one another, as God in Christ has forgiven you" (Ephesians 4:32).

Confession as part of worship is normally followed with absolution. All of us are invited to confess—lay and clergy alike. The forgiveness that comes through absolution is a gift that God gives to us and that we then share with ourselves and with one another.

Be Transparent in Communication

No one knows what another person is thinking until that person speaks or writes. Words are the way we share our thoughts. Once uttered, words can never be taken back. They enter the realm of the public forever. In the book of James, we are warned that the tongue "is a fire. . . . From the same mouth come blessing and cursing" (James 3:6–10). Therefore, communication needs to be handled very carefully; a reflective silence is often better than a thoughtless word. We must be clear in all we say and write. We can't hide behind flowery phrases and convoluted sentences. We must think about our message and meaning and strive for clarity and honesty. We are to communicate as much about the joyful and good news as we do about the sad and bad news and provide both context and reason for our communication, including guidance on how the communication can and should be shared.

Think About How the Communication Will Be Received

Christian communities will use a variety of different mediums for communication—the Sunday notices, the e-mails, the letters, and the church meetings. The audience for every communication informs not only the message and meaning but also how it will be perceived. To communicate effectively, we must put ourselves in the readers' shoes. What do they need to know? What previous knowledge do they have? Are there any language barriers or cultural differences to consider? What is their role, and what do we want or need them to do with the information? Will the recipients fail to notice the good news in the midst of our concerns? Or will they miss the bad news hidden between the meaningless commentary? We must strive to communicate the same message, even if everyone is reading it from their own experience and perspective.

Be Considerate—It Is Part of Christian E-mail Etiquette

Let's get really practical. E-mail is a primary means of communication in our modern world. It disappears from our screen, and we trust it arrives quickly. A few seconds, perhaps minutes, lapse. There are a few basics of Christian e-mail etiquette. We must be thoughtful in the construction of the e-mail. We should use a salutation for politeness, and we should be timely in our responses. E-mail must never be written in haste or rage. Sleep on the angry e-mail, and even after that, run the text past a friend or spouse before sending the message. Civility in our e-mail correspondence is a key part of living in community.

Our Social Media Presence Needs to Reflect Grace and Gospel

Social media is a fabulous tool for evangelism and communication, but before we snap, tweet, post, or share, we must remember Rules 1 through 6. Also consider Rule 11. It can be great to post a photo of a recent baptism, but did we first think about our responsibilities to protect children? Is Facebook Live our best tool for sharing that awesome prophetic sermon we preached, or would a single snap be a better medium? And don't forget that others are snapping, tweeting, and sharing about us. Let us be mindful that all we say and do is meant to enhance the body of Christ and to further the coming of God's realm on earth.

5 ▪ What's Old Is New Again

Clearly, there is much we can do to improve our effectiveness with new media as both tools and locales for renewing Christian community.

These are still early days in the Digital Reformation, so no one has it exactly right. But the practices of listening, attending, connecting, and engaging that draw from our deepest traditions can move effectively from face-to-face to digital settings.

The Digital Reformation invites us back to ways of relating, sharing, and creating meaning together that were all but lost as the sweep of modern progress moved into the Broadcast Age. While these social technologies can often seem impossibly complicated, the core practices they encourage are not far off from those that animated medieval faith communities. These practices—listening, attending, connecting, engaging—form a kind of "lace" that symbolizes the interaction among the fundamental spiritual practices of the Digital Reformation.

Woven through broader categories of communication, community, and leadership practice are more subtle practices of listening, attending, connecting, and engaging that might be imagined as something like a Celtic Trinity knot. The dynamic, relational interplay symbolized by the Trinity lace is part of our deepest theology and spirituality as Christians—our habitus.

Listening

The Greek philosopher Epictetus gave us the adage: "We have two ears and one mouth so that we can listen twice as much as we speak." This wisdom applies as much in digital space as in physical space. As we'll see, you're not a creepy stalker if you take some time to visit the Facebook pages, Twitter feeds, blogs, and websites of the people in your digital networks. You're getting to know people, and you're getting to know the lay of the digital landscape you inhabit with them.

People put up pictures and list their interests because they want other people to see how they see themselves and the worlds they inhabit. It's okay to look at the groups people "like" on Facebook or the lists they follow on Twitter. It's fine to click on the "information" tab and see what people have decided to share about their education or their job. It's totally cool to watch the video they posted of their vacation or their daughter's graduation—not by way of gathering marketing data, but by way of trying to understand what matters to them. If you've ever said to someone at coffee hour, "Tell me a little bit about yourself," you know exactly how to do this.

Attending

Listening is part of attending, but it's not the whole of it. "To attend," beyond the standard dictionary definition of "paying attention to," means "to be present with," "to notice," "to be ready for service or ministry to." In the digital world, attending can be as simple as clicking "like" on someone's Facebook page. A lot of attending comes down to just being polite and kind in digital space in the same do-as-you-would-have-others-do ways you would want to practice in a face-to-face setting. The digital version of Paul's repeated instruction that we "greet each other with a holy kiss" (Romans 16:16, 1 Corinthians 16:20, 2 Corinthians 13:12, 1 Thessalonians 5:26) seems to play out in these small gestures, as well as in the microethical digital practices of honesty and acknowledgment when reposting or retweeting material you found on someone else's page. Especially for leaders in ministry, this digital attentiveness powerfully models Christian love of neighbor in an environment where many people rightly worry (though often overmuch) about declining moral standards.

Connecting

In the world of social networking, "connecting" is usually where people want to start. On Facebook, connecting is more or less a requirement if you're going to be able to listen or attend to anyone. On Twitter, you can "follow" anyone you want, and many of the kindest among them will follow you back. The trick in either case is not to set yourself up like Socrates, tweeting and posting your wisdom and waiting for disciples to gather around you. Jesus invited children to gather around him (Matthew 19:13–15), but he pretty much hoofed it out to everyone else. Even the Sermon on the Mount (Matthew 5:1–7:29) was part of an extended road trip that allowed Jesus to encounter people he didn't already know.

As it turns out, in the social media world (as in the rest of life), whoever amasses the largest number of friends and followers does not "win." Still, it is a huge part of the vocations of people who understand themselves as leaders in ministry to ensure that everyone who asks has a place at the table, digital or otherwise. Social media platforms don't invite the development of exclusive cocktail parties. They're more like pickup games in a giant, global park. Everybody gets to play, though there's nothing wrong with helping people to figure out what spot is best suited to their interests and gifts. Connecting as generously as we are reasonably able expresses an important spiritual value to fellow travelers in the Digital Reformation.

Engaging

Appropriate practices of listening, attending, and connecting ground meaningful engagement in social media contexts in the same ways they do in face-to-face settings. Once you understand the interests of people in your core network, sharing content that is meaningful to them enriches relationship. One of the valuable lessons we learned from the medieval mystic Julian of Norwich, who could see the whole of God's creation in something as small as a hazelnut, applies here: less is very often more. Sometimes—especially when you're discerning how many tweets and Facebook posts to log in a day—it's everything.

All of this is part of a practice of participating in social media spaces by way of building relationships that deepen and extend community rather than messaging or marketing your church, organization, or cause. People want to be known, and they want to know you—personally, not institutionally.

6 ▪ Grounded in Prayer

It's one thing to find a place for prayer, even a type of prayer. Doing it daily, not unlike exercise, is the difficult part. To maintain a life of prayer akin to breathing is every disciple's goal, yet it remains out of reach for most of us. In part, maintaining a healthy prayer life is difficult because we fall away so quickly. It is easy to let the day's interruptions take charge, and so little by little we drift away from a sustainable and sustaining routine. But we need to do the work: identify a place, carve out a time, and commit. If you have tried it before, return to it yet again. Living in the fellowship of the saints is predominately a work of prayer. You will find it so much more difficult to engage in kingdom building if you are not building on a strong foundation of prayer. Being mindful and prayerful is not just something you do while locked away in secret. Prayer is for all of life, so have courage and bring prayer into yours. Feel free to pray in the car, in your office, at your dinner table, with your children, with friends, before a meeting, after a meeting. The Holy Spirit, which seeks to unite us with God, also opens our hearts and eyes to discover God in our world. Prayer tunes you to see and be aligned with the Spirit.

The Rule of the Society of Saint John the Evangelist (SSJE), an Episcopal monastic community, states that by praying throughout our life we see how we can "be available to God in the present moment." Over time, we see that "prayer comes to permeate our life and transfigure our mundane routines." We are in some very real way, when we choose to follow Jesus, choosing not simply to learn to pray, but to pray as we live.

Jesus's Prayer

In the Episcopal Church, the Lord's Prayer—the prayer Jesus taught his disciples—is central to our common life of prayer. It is present in all of our private and corporate services of worship, and it is often the first prayer children learn. With the simplest of words, Jesus teaches those who follow him all they need to know about prayer.

Our Father

Our Father, because we are to seek as intimate a relationship with God as Jesus did. We can develop this intimate love with God, recognizing we are children of God and members of the family of God.

Who art in heaven

We are reminded of our created nature as a gift from heaven. Life is given to us from God, who is quite beyond us. We recognize in this short phrase that we are not God. Rather, the God we proclaim is a God who makes all things and breathes life into all things.

Hallowed be thy name

In response to the grace of being welcomed into God's community, bowing humbly and acknowledging our created nature, we recognize the holiness of God. We proclaim that God's name is hallowed.

Thy kingdom come

We ask and seek God's kingdom. The words of Jesus remind us that, like the disciples' own desires to sit at the right and left hand of Jesus, this is not our kingdom. The reign of God is not what you and I have in mind. We beg, "God, by your power bring your kingdom into this world. Help us to beat our swords into plowshares that we might feed the world. Give us strength to commit as your partners in the restoration of creation, not how we imagine it, but in the way you imagine it."

Thy will be done

We bend our wills to God's, following the living example of Jesus Christ. We ask for grace to constantly set aside our desires and take on the love of God's reign. We pray, "Let our hands and hearts build not powers and principalities but the rule of love and care for all sorts and conditions of humanity. Let us have a measure of wisdom to tear down our self-imposed walls and embrace one another, as the lion and the lamb lay down together in the kingdom of God."

On earth as it is in heaven

We ask God to give us eyes to see this kingdom vision, and then we ask for courage and power to make heaven a reality in this world. We pray to God, "Create in us a will to be helping hands and loving hearts for those who are weary and need to rest in you.

May our homes, our churches, and our communities be a sanctuary for the hurting world to find shelter, to find some small experience of heaven."

Give us this day our daily bread

In prayer we come to understand that we are consumers. We need, desire, and just want many things. In Christ, we are reminded that all we need is our daily bread. So we pray, "O God, help us to be mindful that you provide for the lilies of the field and you provide for us. As we surrender our desires, help us to provide daily bread for those who have none today."

Forgive us our trespasses, as we forgive those who trespass against us

Sanity and restoration are possible only because God forgives us. Because of that sacrificial forgiveness—made real in the life and death of Jesus—we can see and then share mercy and forgiveness. Then we can pray, "God, may I understand your call to me personally to offer sacrificial forgiveness to all those I feel have wronged me. I want to know and see my own fault in those broken relationships. May I be the sacrament of your grace and forgiveness to others."

Lead us not into temptation

As Adam and Eve ate from the tree of knowledge and replaced God with their own understanding of reality, we need help turning away from our own earthly and political desires and turning toward the wisdom of God in Christ Jesus. So we ask, "We are so tempted to go the easy way, to believe our desires are God's desires. We have the audacity to assume we can know God's mind. Show us your way and help us to trust it."

Deliver us from evil

Only God can deliver us from evil. There is darkness in the world around us. We know this darkness feeds on our deepest desire: to be God ourselves. That deceptive voice affirms everything we do and justifies our actions, even when they compromise other people's dignity. It whispers and tells us we possess God's truth and no one else does. We must pray, "God, deliver us from the evil that inhabits this world, the weakness of our hearts, and the darkness of our lives, that we might walk in the light of your Son."

For thine is the kingdom, and the power, and the glory, for ever and ever. Amen.

Without God, we are powerless. So, we devote our lives to God, resting in the power of God's deliverance. We humbly ask, "Help us to see your glory and beauty in the world, this day and every day. Amen."

Using prayers like this one, Jesus modeled a life of prayer as work, and work as prayer. The apostles and all those who have since followed him have sought a life of prayer. They have engaged in prayer that discerns Jesus' teachings and then molded their lives into the shape of his life. We can take up the same vocation and become people whose lives are characterized by daily and fervent prayer. We reflect and acknowledge the centrality of prayer and work in our own commitment to God when we say, "I will, with God's help, continue in the apostles' teaching and fellowship, in the breaking of bread, and in the prayers."

Entering God's Community

God is united in an infinite exchange of love: Father, Son, and Holy Spirit. This is the very simplest way of understanding the divine union we call the Trinity. Prayer is not, in its very nature, simply a conversation with God. When we pray, we participate in the divine life of love, the divine community, the divine conversation. As God's creatures, we become entangled in the embrace of God. Through prayer we are lifted into the community of God. In this embrace, the idea of praying to or worshiping a foreign or "distant" God disappears. We are overcome by the grace of being invited into the divine union of God, and as a result our own adoration and thanksgiving well up and pour out.

Prayer is sacramental—a visible, physical sign filled with an invisible grace, a tangible link between us and Jesus. In it we discover again and again that we are members of God's body, tied to both the community of the Trinity and to the community of the faithful. When we pray, God hears the voice of Jesus in our prayers and accepts them as his own.

Especially when we bring intercessions for others to this communal God, we discover a deep and abiding kinship. We pray for family, friends, coworkers, clergy, and fellow church members. God is at work in these prayers; our voices are part of Christ's voice raising each person to God. Our prayers for those among us who are poor, widowed, sick, homeless, lonely, or lost bridge the chasm between us all and send us out, empowered by the Holy Spirit, to work for healing and reconciliation, forgiveness and restoration. Our prayer also leads us to help people discover their own vocations. We are guides along the way, listening with people and helping them to listen for God as they discern their own unique callings into ministry. If we are following Jesus, then prayer must be the origin of our work. This is the way we come to know our place within the community of God. This is the way God's community comes alive on earth.